JOHN THOMPSON'S
EASIEST PIANO COUR

GW00673742

EASIEST SMASH HITS

This collection of smash hits is intended as supplementary material for those working through **John Thompson's Easiest Piano Course** Parts One to Three. The pieces may also be used for sight-reading practice by more advanced students.

Dynamics have been deliberately omitted from the earlier pieces, since they are not introduced until Part Three of the Easiest Piano Course, and initially the student's attention should be focused on playing notes and rhythms accurately. Outline fingering has been included, and in general the hand is assumed to remain in a five-finger position until a new fingering, in the later pieces, indicates a position shift. The fingering should suit most hands, although logical alternatives are always possible.

ISBN: 978-1-70510-803-1

WILLIS MUSIC

EXCLUSIVELY DISTRIBUTED BY

HAL•LEONARD®

Visit Hal Leonard Online at
www.halleonard.com

Contact us:
Hal Leonard
7777 West Bluemound Road
Milwaukee, WI 53213
Email: info@halleonard.com

In Europe, contact:
Hal Leonard Europe Limited
42 Wigmore Street
Marylebone, London, W1U 2RY
Email: info@halleonardeurope.com

In Australia, contact:
Hal Leonard Australia Pty. Ltd.
4 Lentara Court
Cheltenham, Victoria, 3192 Australia
Email: info@halleonard.com.au

Havana

Words and Music by CAMILA CABELLO, LOUIS BELL, PHARRELL WILLIAMS, ADAM FEENEY, ALI TAMPOSI,
JEFFERY LAMAR WILLIAMS, BRIAN LEE, ANDREW WOTMAN, BRITTANY HAZZARD, and KAAN GUNESBERK

Count on Me

Words and Music by BRUNO MARS, ARI LEVINE, and PHILIP LAWRENCE

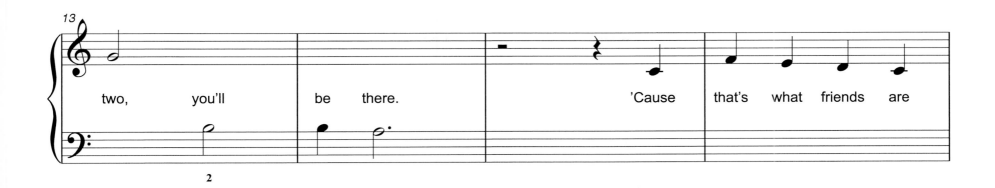

two,　　you'll　　be　there.　　　　　　　　　　'Cause　that's　what　friends　are

2

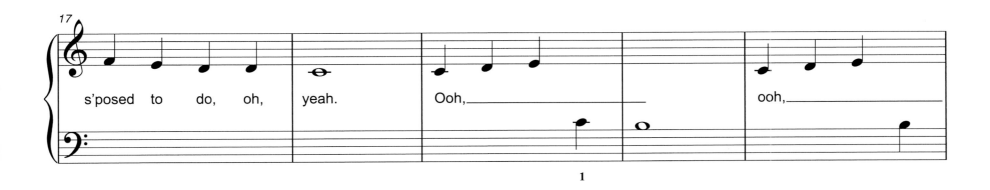

s'posed　to　do,　oh,　yeah.　　Ooh,＿＿＿＿＿＿　　　　　ooh,＿＿＿＿＿

1

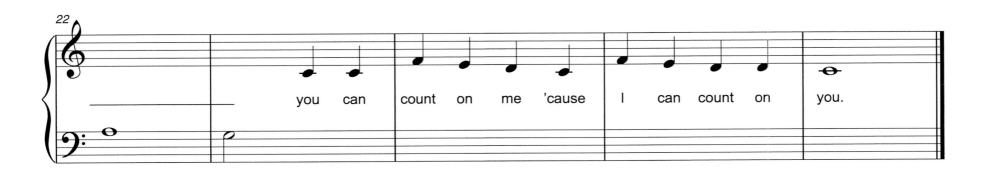

＿＿＿＿＿　you　can　count　on　me　'cause　I　can　count　on　you.

All Is Found
from the film FROZEN 2

Music and Lyrics by KRISTEN ANDERSON-LOPEZ and ROBERT LOPEZ

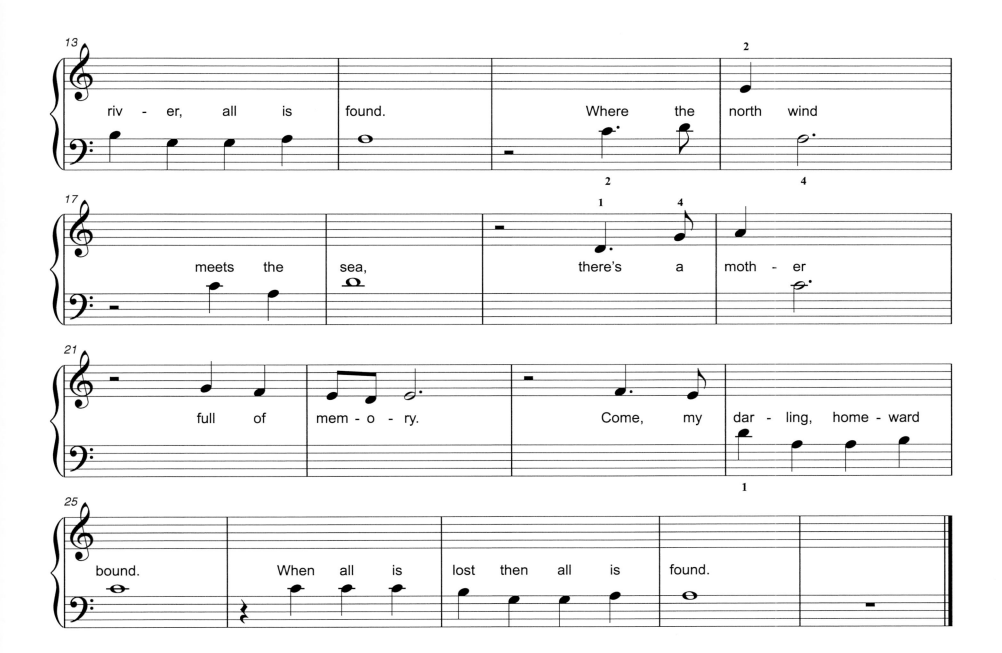

Shallow
from the film A STAR IS BORN

Words and Music by STEFANI GERMANOTTA, MARK RONSON,
ANDREW WYATT, and ANTHONY ROSSOMANDO

Powerfully

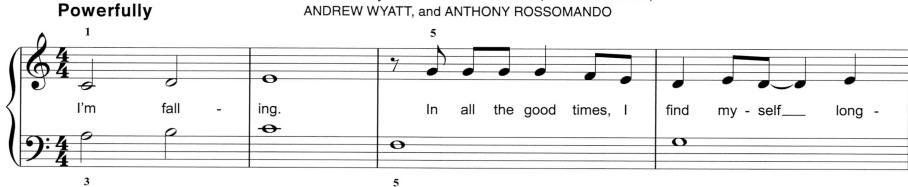

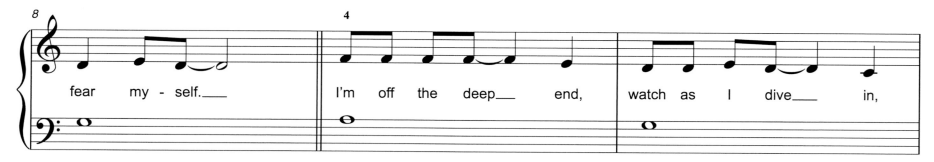

Old Town Road (I Got the Horses in the Back)

Words and Music by TRENT REZNOR, ATTICUS ROSS, KIOWA ROUKEMA, and MONTERO LAMAR HILL

Ploddingly

Sign of the Times

Words and Music by HARRY STYLES, JEFF BHASKER, MITCH ROWLAND, RYAN NASCI, ALEX SALIBIAN, and TYLER JOHNSON

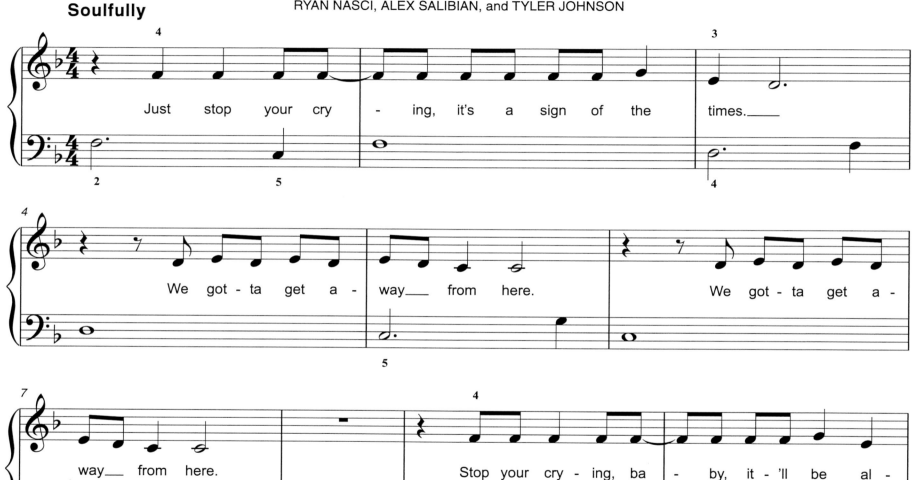

Dynamite

Words and Music by TAIO CRUZ, LUKASZ GOTTWALD, MAX MARTIN, BENJAMIN LEVIN, and BONNIE MCKEE

15

Get Back Up Again

from the film TROLLS

Words and Music by JUSTIN PAUL and BENJ PASEK

A Thousand Years

from the Summit Entertainment film THE TWILIGHT SAGA: BREAKING DAWN – PART 1

Words and Music by DAVID HODGES and CHRISTINA PERRI

A Million Dreams
from the film THE GREATEST SHOWMAN

Words and Music by BENJ PASEK and JUSTIN PAUL

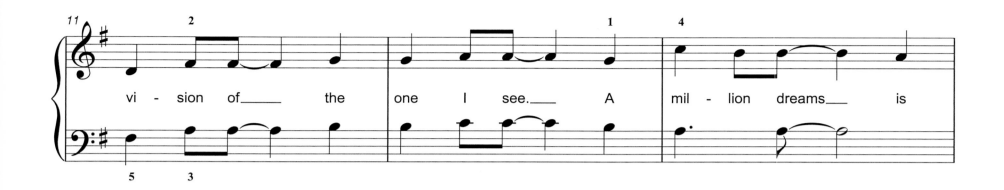

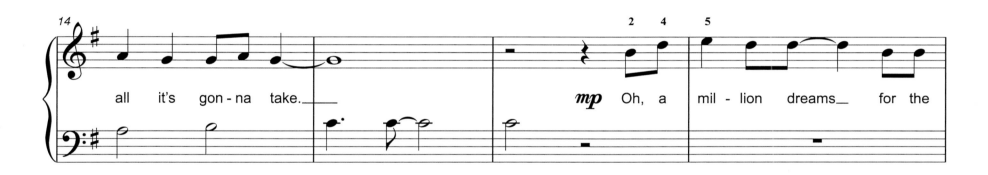

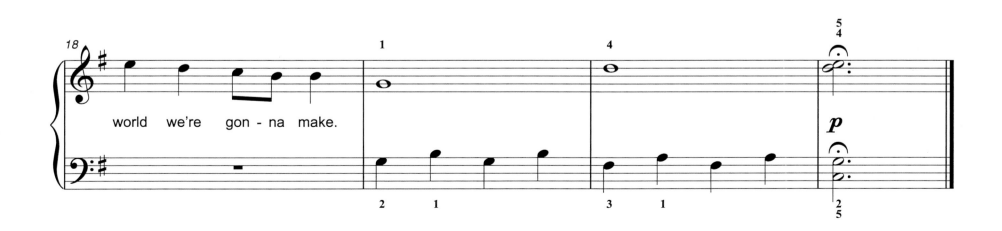

Firework

Words and Music by KATY PERRY, MIKKEL ERIKSEN,
TOR ERIK HERMANSEN, ESTHER DEAN, and SANDY WILHELM

Shotgun

Words and Music by GEORGE BARNETT,
JOEL LASLETT POTT, and FRED GIBSON

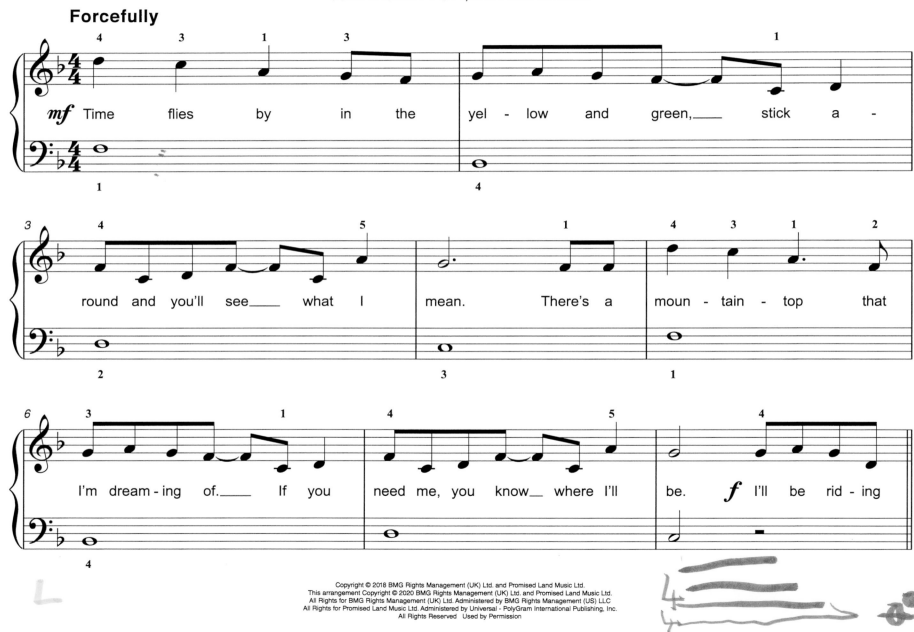

Ocean Eyes

Words and Music by FINNEAS O'CONNELL

Someone You Loved

Words and Music by LEWIS CAPALDI, BENJAMIN KOHN,
PETER KELLEHER, THOMAS BARNES, and SAMUEL ROMAN

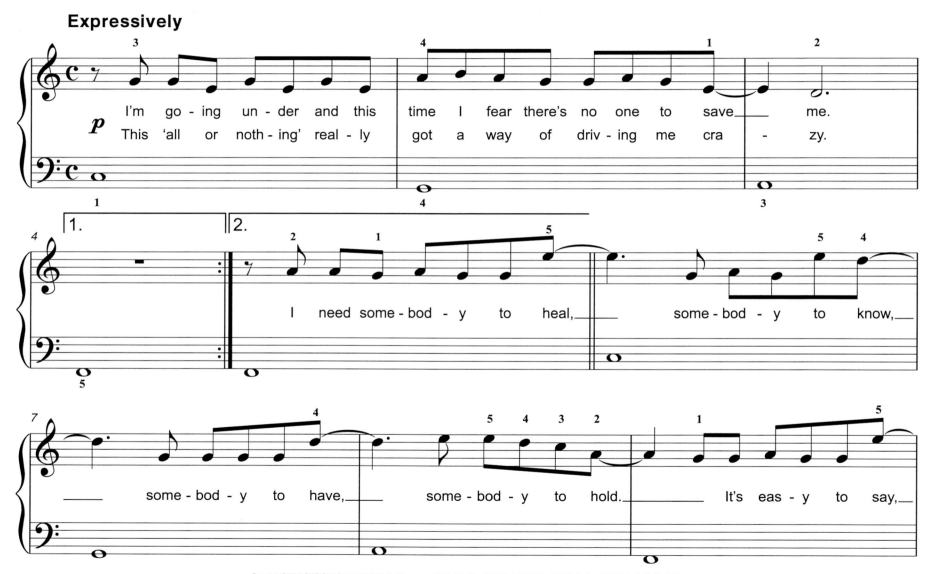

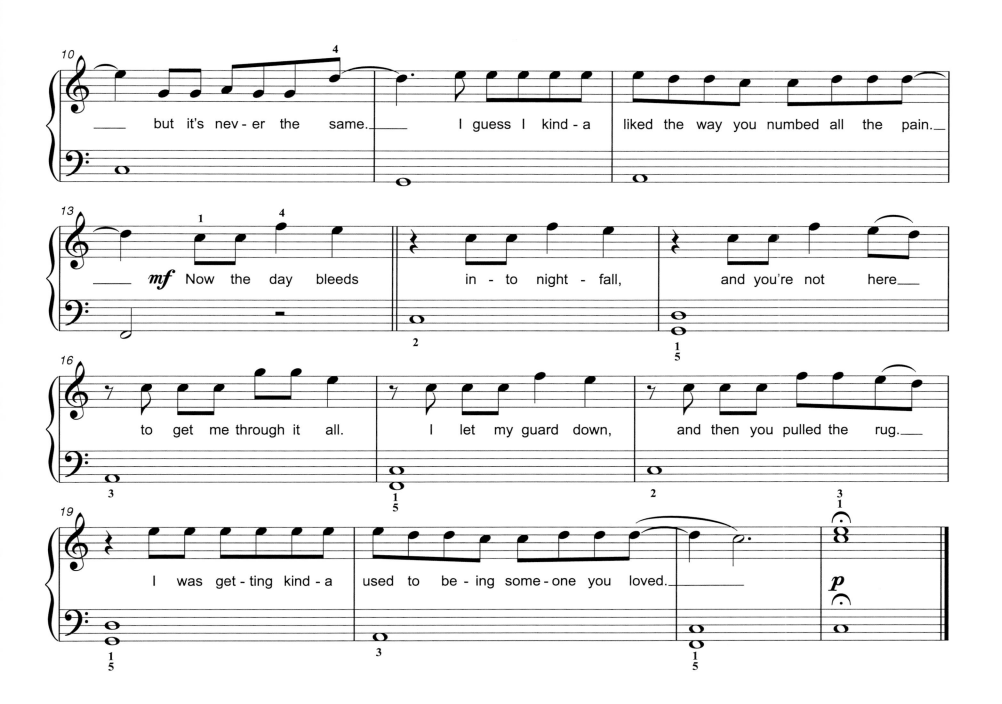

Perfect

Words and Music by ED SHEERAN

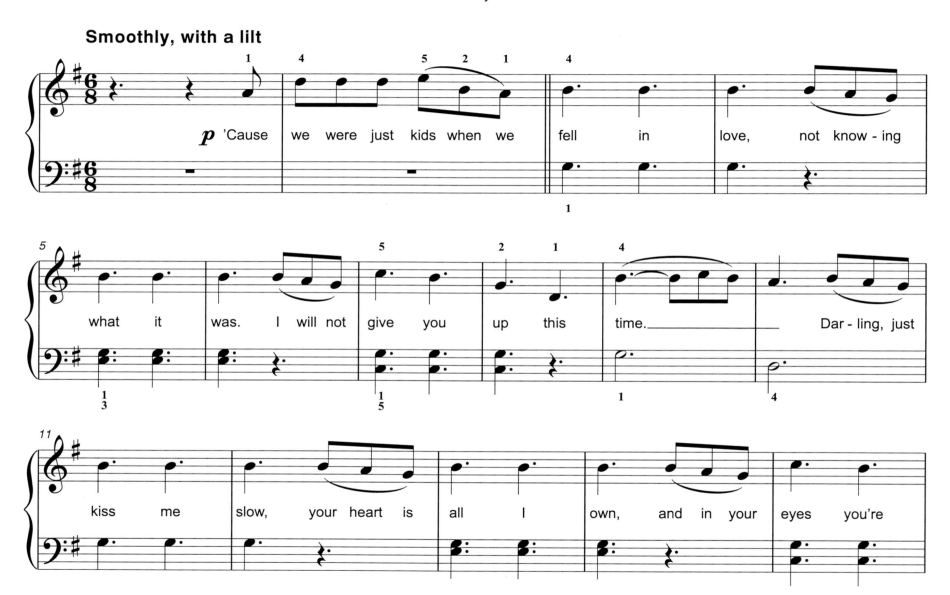

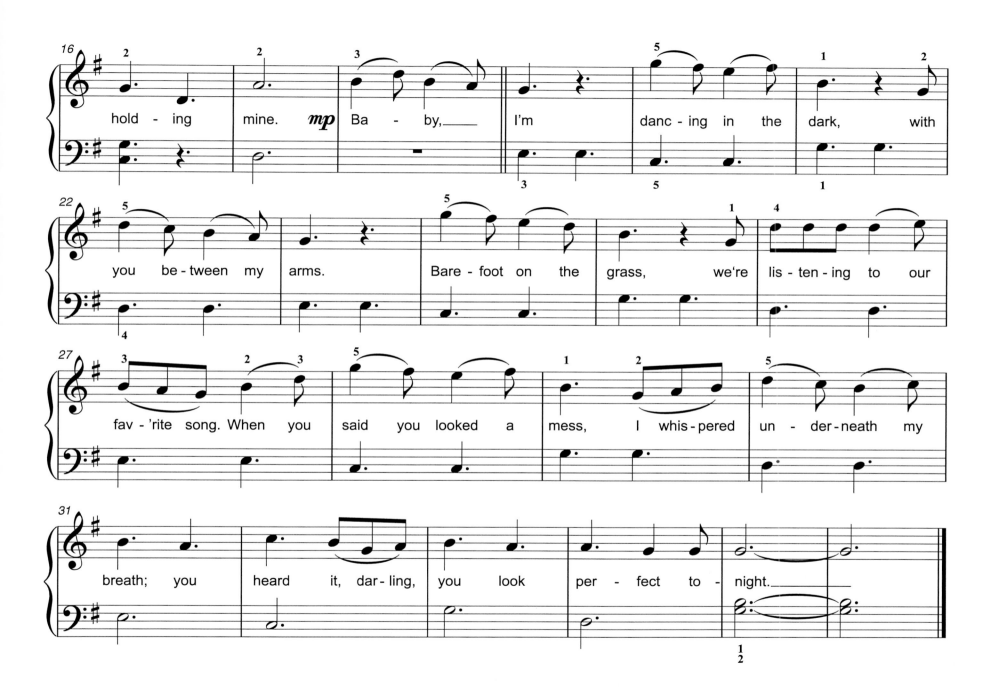